UNHEARD VOICES: FINALLY HEARD

TALES OF COMPASSION AND CHANGE

EMPATHETIC HUMANS

This book is dedicated to the **power of giving**, which can ignite remarkable transformations in people's lives.

Contents

Preface

As the New Year brings joy and happiness to many, it's essential to remember those whose lives remain unchanged, year after year. In 2024, we had the opportunity to provide financial support to those in need, helping them take steps toward progress and stability. We embraced this chance to make a lasting difference in their lives.

This book is a continuation of our first book, '**The Unheard Voices of Mundhwa**' which made us realize the everyday problems in our community which we usually overlook. While writing it, we felt a mix of emotions: sadness, empathy, and a strong urge to help. The stories shared by 45 young co-authors were like snapshots of real life, showing the struggles street vendors go through. These stories were like a mirror, showing us things we might not have wanted to see. But now, we're left wondering, "How can we truly be a light in their darkness?" While identifying the problem is one thing, finding a meaningful solution is far more challenging.

Eventually, our book caught the attention of someone who shares our passion for helping others and understanding their struggles. His name is **Mr. Vittorio Lim**, and he is from the Philippines. He helps needy people in his own country. While staying at the Taj Hotel in Mumbai during his trip to India, he came across our book. We were amazed because we never imagined our book would reach such a prestigious place. After reading it, he reached out to us via email, expressing his desire to support the people we interviewed by investing 1 lakh rupees. It was a surprising and heartwarming gesture that left us deeply grateful. We were grateful that a stranger trusted us with such a significant financial responsibility.

We held ourselves accountable to use the money wisely to help those who need it, but the biggest challenge was making sure this money was used well. We weren't sure how people would use it. At first, we thought about giving out food to struggling people, but we realized that wouldn't solve the problem in the long term. So we came up with the idea to hand over the funds to the person who could create a sustainable cycle of money. The people who could start or expand their small business with it and grow from it, so they wouldn't just have food on their plates for a day but every day.

When we started looking for people who needed help, some of us were lucky to find the same people we interviewed for our first book, but for others, it was hard to find the same individuals. Maybe they had moved to another place or shifted their place of business. Since we are all in junior college, we have explored places other than Mundhwa and saw many people struggling throughout the streets of Pune. So, we decided to focus on interviewing them. Even though we felt disappointed when people didn't want our help or when they didn't fit our profile, we kept trying. Finally, after several failed attempts, we found the right people in need.

Within a couple of days, 1 lakh rupees arrived in our mentor's account. When we began brainstorming how to distribute the money, it posed a challenge. If we handed 6,000 rupees each to 15 identified people, we wouldn't know how they'd use it, nor could we witness their progress. So, instead of giving the full amount upfront, we decided on two instalments of 3,000 rupees each. To make the process easier, we explained to the people we interviewed that we would conduct weekly visits to receive detailed updates on how the funds had been effectively utilized. This approach not only made the process smoother but also built trust between us and the recipients.

After three months of tracking their progress, we began our journey to document these stories of transformation. Along the way, we learned numerous lessons and gained a reality check about the world, which you'll notice in our chapters. Each chapter is written by one of our co-authors, reinforcing the importance of helping others.

About Us

Empathetic Humans is our group name. We are a group of 15 students who have just completed our 11th grade and are co-authors of the book 'The Unheard Voices of Mundhwa'. United by our compassion and drive to make a difference, we embarked on a journey to shed light on the struggles of marginalized communities. Through our collective effort, we have documented real-life stories that reveal the unseen challenges faced by street vendors and other underprivileged individuals. Our work not only highlights these issues but also strives to find practical solutions to improve the lives of those in need. Together, we form a team dedicated to empathy, understanding, and social impact, using our voices and actions to bring about meaningful change.

Contact Us

We would love to connect with you and hear your thoughts, feedback and actions that we together could take to address the social problems. Shoot us an email at: **empathetichumans@gmail.com**

Acknowledgements

This book reflects our journey of stepping out of our comfort zone, expanding our horizons, and reaching out to those facing hardship.

First and foremost, we want to express our deepest gratitude to the 15 co-authors for their courage and empathy throughout this journey. By reaching out to those in need, they not only listened but brought their powerful stories of change to life. Their dedication to telling these unheard voices with compassion is what made this book possible. Without their unwavering commitment, this remarkable work would not have come to fruition.

1. Aaniya Shaikh
2. Aarti Sharma
3. Anushka Mishra
4. Kanchan Kol
5. Nitesh Yadav
6. Pooja Bodekar
7. Pooja Gupta
8. Prajakta Gaud
9. Rachana Mali
10. Samruddhi More
11. Sanskruti Badgujar
12. Saurabh Verma
13. Shraddha Singh
14. Suhani Dwivedi
15. Tejaswee Hole

We would also like to acknowledge the invaluable contributions of the five young editors who worked tirelessly to enhance and refine the stories. Pooja Gupta, Nitesh Yadav, Shraddha Singh, Anushka Mishra, and Aarti Sharma, your dedication and attention to detail have truly elevated the quality of this book.

A big thanks to our young project manager, **Saurabh Verma**, for keeping us accountable to agreed timelines throughout this project. His dedication to his role made sure that every task was completed on time and with the utmost precision. His leadership was crucial in guiding our team to success.

We would also like to extend our heartfelt gratitude to **Ms. Namita Agarwal, Ms. Gargi Mishra**, and **Ms. Arefa Bootwala** for taking the time to review and provide thoughtful feedback on our manuscript. Their insights and suggestions helped shape the final version of this book, enhancing both its narrative and impact. Their careful attention to detail and encouragement played a crucial role in bringing this project to completion.

This book would not have come to fruition without the financial support and inspiration from **Mr. Vittorio Lim** from the Philippines. He not only reached out to congratulate us on our first book but also expressed his willingness to support our interviewees financially. His suggestion to cover these stories in our second book reignited our desire to help our interviewees and paved the way for this remarkable endeavor.

Special thanks to **Ms. Suchita Mohan** for her invaluable support throughout this project. Not only did she patiently review our manuscript and provide insightful feedback, but she also offered her expertise in the cover design process, ensuring it resonated with our vision. Her constant check-ins on our progress motivated us to stay focused and dedicated. Her holistic approach and commitment to enhancing the structure of the book were instrumental in bringing our collective vision to life.

Lastly, but most importantly, this book would be incomplete without acknowledging one person: our motivator, and mentor, **Mr. Aman Gupta**. His guidance and belief in us have been invaluable. He was the one who saw an opportunity after Vittorio Lim's email, brought us all together, pitched and convinced us of the idea for the second book, brainstormed a project plan, and trusted us to execute it with excellence. This book would neither have started nor been completed without his vision and commitment.

Part I: Silent Sacrifices

CHAPTER ONE

UNDESIRED PATH OF LIFE

-By Tejaswee Hole

"In the shadows of society, untold tales of hardship and struggle endure, unseen and unheard, reminding us of the profound depths of human resilience amidst the darkest of realities."

Our first book, "Unheard Voices of Mundwa," was a life-changing moment for me. The stories in it moved me deeply, making me believe even more that, everyone deserves to be treated with kindness and fairness. Reading about the real struggles people face showed me how unique and tough each person's journey is. When I heard about our new project, I felt a rush of excitement.

I felt nervous about the many challenges ahead, with countless questions swirling in my mind. Who should I help? Where could I find someone who truly needed assistance? Then my mother mentioned a woman she knew who was in need. I tried to find her a lot but eventually gave up, feeling even more upset. One dark night, burdened by a lot of questions, I went for a walk. By chance, I saw that woman walking on the same path as me, the woman I had been searching for a long time. Overjoyed, I approached her and started talking. "I was looking for you for a long time, where were you? Literally, I gave up!" Then I realized I forgot to introduce myself, so I did and explained why I was looking for her. At first, she was wary and asked, "Why should I trust a stranger with my personal life?" After sharing my intentions and meeting my mother, whom she knew, she was convinced.

I asked her about her hardships and listened closely to her story. She told me about her struggles, and I could see the pain in her eyes. Meeting someone who truly needed help touched my heart deeply. All my earlier feelings of helplessness melted away, replaced by a strong sense of purpose. Knowing I could help her filled me with joy and satisfaction. Watching her receive the support she desperately needed was incredibly heartwarming. It made me realize that even when life is tough, there are always chances to make a positive difference in someone else's life.

Mrs. Shobha Joseph

Meet Shobha Joseph. She is the only support for her family, which includes her mother and her 12-year-old son. Shobha got married at 16 without any education or money. Her husband left her when their son was just 2 years old. Six years later, her father died, leaving Shobha feeling lonely, broken, and lost. Her brother wasn't supportive, but Shobha didn't give up. She searched everywhere for a job until she finally found work as a household worker. Every day, she worked many jobs to provide for her family and make sure her son could go to school. Despite her hard work, she barely earned enough to cover their basic needs, always struggling to make ends meet. Even with these challenges, Shobha stays strong and determined. She dreams of a brighter future for her mother and son and works tirelessly to make it happen. Her perseverance and dedication are truly inspiring. Shobha proves that even in the face of overwhelming odds, hope and hard work can lead to a better life. Hearing her story makes one feel grateful for their own advantages and deeply empathetic towards Shobha. She faces so many hardships alone, without anyone to share her burdens, yet she never stops fighting for her family. Shobha's journey is a powerful reminder that strength and determination can overcome even the toughest challenges.

"Hardship may bend her, but it has never broken the never-say-die spirit to overcome."

I handed her the envelope of money, and her joy was clear. She couldn't find the right words, but her heartfelt "Thank you" showed how grateful she was. The shine in her eyes told me how much the help meant to her. At that moment, I felt a deep sense of happiness and pride, knowing that our support had truly changed her life. Tears filled my eyes as I realized the big impact of this small act of kindness. This experience showed me that even simple acts of kindness can bring hope and joy to others.

Every 3 to 4 days, I started visiting her home. During my initial visit, I saw her humble home for the first time. It was a modest, 80-square-foot room fitted out with basic amenities like utensils, a single cupboard, and a couch. In spite of its limited space, she skillfully arranged all her household belongings and comfortably housed her family within its confines.

Initially, she spent some of the money on her mother's hospital treatment. Later, during another visit, she revealed that she had used a portion of the funds for her own medical expenses. Because of financial issues, she hadn't been able to afford treatment before. She spent two days in the hospital due to some minor health issues. Reflecting on her experiences, she shared how hard it is to live in such conditions and the sacrifices she made for her family's well-being. Despite the challenges, she's determined to give her family a better life.

She'd use the rest of the money for her son's education—paying for school fees, tutors, and books. It's really tough to understand how they live, but her strength and love for her family shine through in everything she does.

After a couple of days, I handed her the second instalment, the extreme joy on her face was immeasurable, and her emotions were clearly visible. It was evident that this moment meant a lot to her, as she hadn't felt this happy ever. With tears welling in her eyes, she expressed her heartfelt gratitude, admitting the impact our help had on her and her family. I gently reminded her that we were just the messengers, to bring support to her. It's moments like these that truly touch the soul and remind us of the power of compassion.

When I visited her again, she utilised the funds for crucial family necessities such as food, daily requirements, transportation, hospitality, and her son's educational expenses (School fees, coaching fees, study stuff and material, etc). Being a household worker, she cannot invest money in business or anything else because she lacks both the necessary skills and knowledge. Therefore, her primary focus is on ensuring her family's well-being and striving for the better quality of life they deserve, while also providing the best education for her son according to her beliefs.

Nowadays, her situation is better than before. It's true that this money will not help her forever; this is temporary help, but a little help shows a huge impact. It gave her the confidence to make better decisions and face life's challenges with more strength and resilience. She's on a brighter path now, and it's inspiring to see how far she's come by facing many challenges. A lot more challenges will come her way, but from now onwards, she will have strong confidence.

> *"Sometimes life takes us to an unwanted path, where we don't desire to walk, but we are forcibly made to follow it. This experience brings out our true character."*

According to my perspective and personal experience, I firmly believe that true happiness can be found in helping others. It's not about whether help is grand or modest in scale; the act itself holds immense value. Helping others is all about genuine intention and the positive impact it has on someone else's life. In extending a helping hand, we not only uplift others but also cultivate a great sense of fulfilment and joy within ourselves.

CHAPTER TWO

Unwavering Hope

-By Prajakta Gaud

Mr. Ganesh Bapu Kamble

I was walking past my college when I noticed a man and an old lady trying to sell stationery items. I had been observing them for a while, and I was intensely curious to learn more about them and their past, simply by watching how hard they worked.

I approached the man and started a casual conversation. Within a few days, we had become friendly, and his manner of speaking made me realize he was a kind person.

Hesitantly, I walked over to him and, with a lot of nervousness, finally asked about taking an interview and explained the entire process. At first, he was a little confused, but then he told me that his name was Mr. Ganesh Bapu Kamble. He lived with his mother, Ms. Malan Bapu Kamble. He had two siblings: an older brother who was married and lived away with his wife and children, and a younger sister who was also married. When I asked about his father, he said that his father had passed away due to illness. He and his mother both worked together. When I asked what he used to do before opening the shop, he said, "I used to sell different types of cooking masalas on the footpath," and also, "I used to deliver newspapers and milk to homes." He even said, "I used to feel so disheartened when people disrespected me or sometimes even spoke rudely while buying things." He continued by saying that after saving money, he opened this small stationery shop, but he still sells masalas from home.

At first, he was a little shocked and hesitant to take the money. He couldn't believe I was actually giving it to him. He initially refused, saying, "It's okay, I don't want it." This showed me what a kind and pure-hearted man he was. But I insisted, urging him to take it. He asked, "Are you really going to give me this money?" I said, "Yes, I brought this money for you." That was the moment his eyes filled with tears and gratitude. He was overwhelmed with emotion and struggled to control himself. I calmed him down and finally handed him the first instalment. He was so happy and showered me with blessings, but he then asked:

"आप हमारी इतनी मदद क्यों कर रहे हो? जबकि अपने भी हमारे लिए इतना नहीं करते जितना आप कर रहे हो।"

(Why are you helping us so much? Even my own people don't do as much for us as you are doing). His lips were trembling as he asked. I told him, "I saw you working hard, honestly, and you were in need. I felt you were the right person to benefit from this fund".

He just smiled at me and told me that he would use the money wisely. At that point, I felt so proud of myself for helping someone who possessed such kindness and selflessness, but who also truly needed the money.

After 3-4 days, I visited him again. He showed me all the things he had bought with it, even showing me the receipts. I was so happy to see that he had used the money responsibly and felt relieved that I had given it to the right person—someone who deserved it. He had bought a bunch of books, a set of geometric compasses, watercolours, and exam papers.

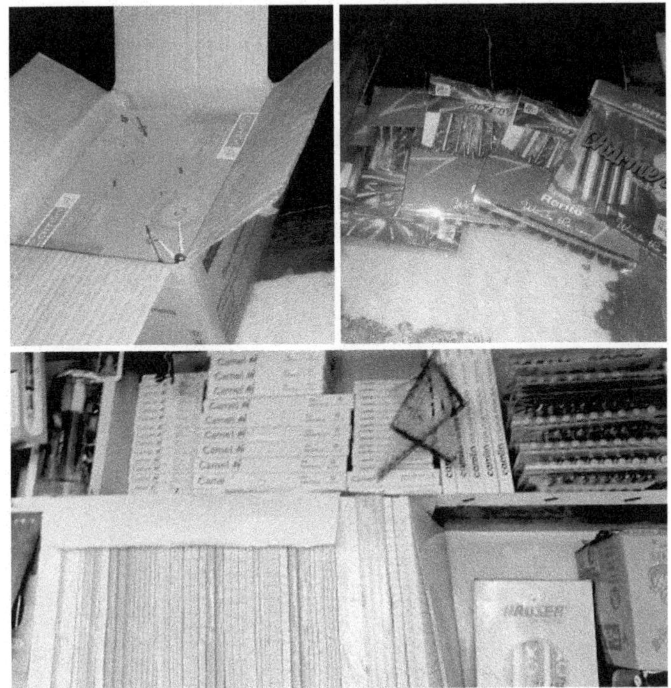

After delivering another instalment, I visited him a little later. When I arrived, he proudly showed me the banner he had made for his masala shop. He said, "This banner cost 2,000 rupees," and even showed me the bill. He used the remaining 1,000 rupees for his mother's medical treatment, as she had been unwell. This time he was even happier because he was able to treat his mother with the money. He thanked me profusely. I felt so satisfied and happy for him because I had not only helped him financially but had also indirectly helped him get his mother the treatment she needed. Her health is now better than before, and I was happy to see her fit and healthy.

I have realised that,

"If we help one another, no one will need luck."

Kindness has no limits: even a small gesture can make a big difference in someone's life. Mr. Ganesh Bapu Kamble's gratitude reminds us how important it is to appreciate the kindness of others.

CHAPTER THREE

GROWTH IS MEANINGLESS WITHOUT STRUGGLES

-By Samruddhi More

Some people work hard, and because of their hard work, we are able to stay safe and clean. They are honest and hardworking individuals, but even so, they are suffering in life because they are uneducated. To feed their families, they often sacrifice their self-respect and work in drains and on the roads. We can only imagine how sad this is, but these things truly happen in their lives. I want to tell the story of a plumber who has faced many hardships, share his experiences, and highlight his efforts for his family. While I am excited to share his story, I also felt sad after hearing about his difficult journey.

Mr. Hawale

He is Mr. Hawale. He was born into an impoverished family. He was only 12 years old when his mother went to work on another farm to feed their family. He grew up in a poor family, and he was only 14 years old when he started selling garlands on the road. Then, to earn more money, he started working as a labourer at a construction site, earning only five hundred rupees for two days, which was really the least amount of money to feed his whole family. Then his friend told him that a relative was looking to hire him as a trainee under a plumber. He agreed, knowing he could learn more and earn extra money by observing the plumber. Over time, he gained enough skills to start his own plumbing business. One of the greatest moments of his life was when he bought his first tool with his own money, a memory that still makes him emotional today.

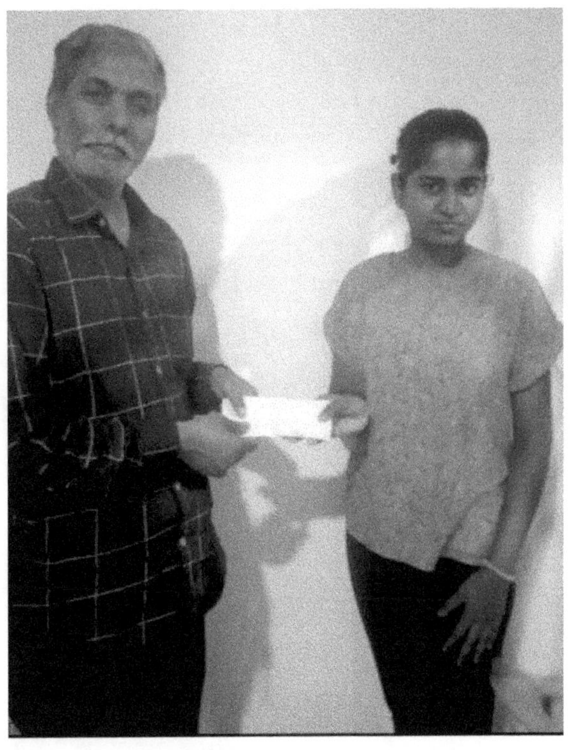

There was no outward expression of emotion, but he was truly thankful to have the money. He was worried about his work because he was getting orders but didn't have enough money to buy some of the tools. Now he could buy those essential tools. The first words that came out of his mouth were "*तुझे खूप खूप आभार*"(Thank you very much). I was on top of the world after hearing those words; I felt proud. He then told me that he would first go to the shop and buy some tools to start work with a new positive spirit, work in a better way, and fulfil his family's needs.

He said that no one had helped him before; they just jeered at him and always made fun of his work. People didn't come near him because he smelt bad after working in the drains. After listening to him, I learned about their painful feelings.

After a few days, he bought a tap and a few tools for his next project. He was grateful that someone understood his struggle and also helped him. He said that no one had helped him with money before. He said that people think plumber work is not difficult; it's just fixing taps and pipes, but he said that he needs to work in drainage and tolerate the horrible smell to earn money. There are a lot of people who have just made fun of him, but he said that to understand someone and also to help someone is a great thing you have done. After listening to this, I feel that we think there are only problems in our own lives, but that's wrong. Other people have problems at a whole other level, problems that are beyond our imagination.

After a few weeks, I went back to his place, and this time I noticed a small smile on his face. He told me that the last instalment had really helped him. He also shared that because of the money, he was earning better and able to feed his family well. He said he was going to buy some new tools and also spend some money on his children's education. He may have limited resources, but he has big dreams. What I admire most is that he is not educated himself, yet he is determined to give his children an education and create a bright future for them. He is working hard to give them the best education so they can achieve something better than he has.

I learned that success will always be within our reach. We just need to work hard and ignore those who try to dominate us and pull us down from our success.

It doesn't matter how much money you have; what truly matters is the purity of your heart and the desire to help others. He is a kind-hearted man, always striving to support his family, friends, and even strangers. His kindness shines through his actions. He works as a plumber but also puts in great effort to fund his daughters' education. He has two daughters—one he hopes will become a lawyer, and the other, a police officer.

Uncle not only supports his immediate family but also helps his sister's and brother's families. He is the kind of person who cares deeply for everyone in his extended family.

This uncle's hard work will definitely culminate in the success of his children. I have realised that,

> "It's not the adversity itself that determines how your life's story will develop, but rather your reaction to it."

CHAPTER FOUR

OVERCOMING ADVERSITY

-By Aaniya Shaikh

When we released our first book 2 years ago, one of the people I interviewed was Uncle Baliraam, a cobbler in Thite Wasti, Kharadi. So, when we started to work on the second book, he was the first person who came to mind. I wanted to see how things had changed for him since our last conversation.

I went to his roadside shop, just like before, and asked him how he was doing. He shared that life was still tough. He has three children—two daughters and a son. His oldest daughter is married, and he's working hard to marry off his second daughter. He also dreams of his son getting a good job to secure his future.

Mr. Baliraam

Seeing his struggles, I wanted to help again. So, I gave Uncle Rs 3000 to support his business. He was really grateful and said he would use the money to buy materials for his work, like socks and supplies to repair shoes. I felt good knowing I could assist him once more.

But later, I realized something—Uncle seemed to have enough to get by, and perhaps my help wasn't as crucial for him as I initially thought. I started to wonder if someone else could make better use of the funds, someone who was in greater need. That's when I decided to shift my focus and help someone whose situation was more urgent.

The next person I chose was Mrs. Shahin, who also lives in Thite Wasti. She has six kids, and her life is much harder. Her eldest daughter is married, and she's trying to get her second daughter married, though she didn't finish school. Her younger daughters are still in school, and her two youngest sons are in LKG and UKG.

Mrs. Shahin

Mrs. Shahin's husband left her two years ago. He used to drink a lot and beat her and the children. She moved to Pune to live with her father, but things didn't get much better. She struggles to provide for her kids, and even getting a place to stay was hard because no one wanted to rent to a woman with so many children. When I visited her, I sat down to ask her about her life. She was surprised and emotional. She said with wet eyes,

"*No one has ever cared to ask about my life before*"

I told her I wanted to help and gave her ₹3000. She was overwhelmed with gratitude and said she would use the money to buy ration for her family and invest in her children's education. Later, she showed me what she had bought: food, school supplies, and basic necessities.

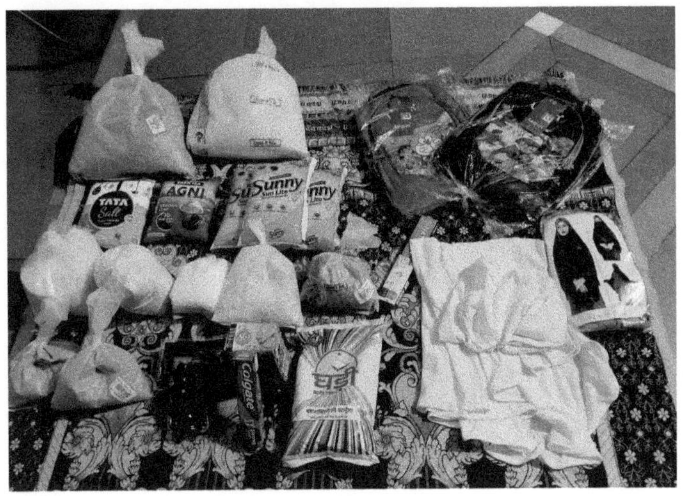

Her ration

Through this experience, I learned the importance of careful consideration before offering help. It's not just about giving—it's about understanding who truly needs it and how it can be used to make a lasting difference. Sometimes, the people we think need the most help are already managing, while others are silently struggling. This taught me that real impact comes from observing closely, asking questions, and then acting wisely.

Part II: Heartaches to Hope

ECHOES OF RESILIENCE

-By Pooja Gupta

Every day while going to my college, I used to see Uncle Suresh working so hard, and it really got me wondering about his life. So one day, I finally gathered up the courage to have a talk with him. I wanted to let Uncle Suresh know why I was so interested in taking the interview and talking to him out of all the people I could have chosen. That's when I showed him the book '**The Unheard Voices of Mundhwa**' that I and my classmates wrote. I explained to him that the book is meant to raise awareness and inspire action, showing how strong and resilient these individuals are. And you know what? Uncle Suresh listened so attentively, his eyes filled with empathy and understanding. He realized that our project aimed to make a real impact beyond just words on a page. And then, he started opening up about his own life.

Uncle Suresh's eyes told a powerful story. They showed a mix of determination and weariness, revealing the daily struggles he faced. He had a difficult childhood, with hunger and lessons learned from his father's farming. Despite all the hardships, he never gave up. He worked tirelessly as a laborer, but faced challenges in his village. Eventually, he lost his job and had to move to Pune, where life continued to be tough. But you know what? He never stopped trying. He kept pushing forward, always striving to give his children a better life. He made sure they stayed with his sister for education, and he would send them money regularly. Uncle Suresh's story is a testament to his strength and love for his family.

As I handed him the money, his eyes brimmed with immense gratitude. He thanked me profusely and assured me that he would utilize the funds to purchase more flowers and toys to sell. Meanwhile, his younger sister sat beside him, diligently crafting garlands of flowers. Her hard work and dedication to supporting their family were truly admirable. Together, they formed an unstoppable team, confronting challenges with resilience and love, a powerful reminder of the strength that can be found within a family working together towards a brighter future.

It had been a long time since anyone had shown him such kindness. In that moment, a mix of emotions washed over him—gratitude, relief, and a glimmer of hope. He was deeply emotional, unable to believe that a stranger like me had selflessly helped him in his time of need. It made him realize that there was still goodness in the world, even when life seemed bleak. The gratitude in the man's eyes warmed my heart and made me feel like I was making a real difference.

He had wisely used the money to purchase hairbands, dustbin bags, and a handkerchief. It was heartwarming to see how a small act of kindness had made such a significant difference in his life. Uncle's eyes filled with tears of gratitude as he looked at me, his voice trembling with emotions. "बेटा, आप मरे लिए भगवान हो। शुक्रिया आपका और आपके सर का।"(Dear, you are like a God to me. Thank you to you and your Sir) he said, his words carrying a deep sense of appreciation. Despite everything, he expressed his heartfelt gratitude and shared his plans to make the best use of the money.

"इस पैसे से मैं और सामान खरीदूंगा, जैसे खिलौने और फूल, ताकि बेहतर तरीके से बेच सकूं"

(With this money I will buy more things, like toys and flowers, so that I can sell them in a better way) he said, a hopeful smile on his face. Uncle's gratitude and commitment deeply touched my heart. It was a privilege to be a part of his journey and witness the positive transformation that unfolded.

I learned that everyone has their own struggles and challenges, even if we can't see them right away. It made me realize the importance of not judging others based on their circumstances. Uncle Suresh's determination and resilience showed me that no matter what life throws at us, we can find the strength to keep going. His story also reminded me of the power of empathy and understanding. It's so important to listen to others and try to understand their experiences. It's stories like his that can inspire us to make a difference in the world.

When I handed him money for the second time, Mr. Suresh was surprised. In that brief moment, his heartfelt gratitude really touched me. He wasn't just thanking me for my help; he was acknowledging the struggles he faced. His resilience in the face of hardship was inspiring, reminding me that we all have the power to make a difference. In the words of Maya Angelou,

"There is no greater agony than bearing an untold story inside you."

Uncle Suresh's story is a testament to the power of sharing experiences and connecting with others. It reminds us that by sharing our own stories, we can inspire and uplift those around us.

CHAPTER SIX

BROKEN FAITH

-By Rachana Mali

I remember my first experience writing our first book. It was one of the reality checks of my life, as I finally confronted the question of why people beg, even when they are physically fit.

At that time, I got to see their pain, but I was very curious and eager to help them. Like a miracle, our understanding of voices reached other empathetic humans in the world, and we got the chance to help our interviewees.

The funds were not just money for me; they were a responsibility, a key to a proper life for someone. There are various types of people who seem like they need help. But it's important to understand that the piece of help you have in your hand is meant for someone specific. I thought it would be easy to find the right person because we now had experience interviewing people and understanding their suffering. But real life was entirely different. This time, just being empathetic was not enough. We had the biggest task of finding the person who really needed the funds the most.

During my initial interview with one cobbler uncle, he candidly shared that his work wasn't about marketing or business expansion. Instead, he emphasized that people would seek his services only when their footwear needed repair and thus won't really grow even with the funds. His straightforward approach left a lasting impression on me—I considered him one of the most genuine individuals I'd ever encountered.

Buoyed by this positive encounter, I continued my quest to connect with others. Armed with a metaphorical bag to collect insights, I conducted six more interviews. However, the task of identifying the person truly in need proved far more challenging than I anticipated. Each interviewee had their unique story, their own struggles, and their genuine suffering. It was akin to solving intricate mathematical problems—each case required careful consideration and empathy.

In the end, I realized that helping others wasn't just about fixing shoes; it was about understanding their lives, their challenges, and their humanity. And sometimes, those complexities made even the most intricate math problems seem straightforward by comparison.

After two days of careful consideration, I made a resolute decision: Mr. Rajan Uncle would be my choice. His humble shop, stocked with basic snacks like '*Kurkure*', might seem unassuming, but it held a story—one that would forever alter my perspective.

Mr. Rajan had a 22-year-old son, his pride and joy. He had invested time and effort in teaching his only child, who eventually earned a computer science degree and secured a job. The arrival of his son's success brought immense happiness to their modest household. Yet, fate can be cruel. On a fateful day, while riding their bike, tragedy struck. An accident snatched away Mr. Rajan's son, leaving him bereaved and hurt. His leg was lost, and with it, a part of his soul. The once vibrant home now echoed with emptiness. Mr. Rajan faced an uphill battle—financially, emotionally, and physically. Desperation led him to sell their family home to fund his son's surgery, but even that sacrifice couldn't restore what was lost. His wife, too, grappled with grief, and together, they wandered through life without a clear vision.

Yet, amidst this darkness, a flicker of determination burned within Mr. Rajan. He refused to surrender entirely. Despite his own physical limitations, he resolved to find a way to serve life. His shop, once a simple snack haven, became a beacon of resilience. With one leg and a heart heavy with sorrow, he continued to greet customers, mend shoes, and offer a listening ear.

In the quiet moments, as he stitched worn-out soles, I realized that Mr. Rajan's journey transcended mere survival. It was about resilience, love, and the relentless pursuit of purpose. His shop wasn't just a place for 'Kurkure'; it was a testament to the human spirit—a reminder that even when life deals its cruelest blows, we can still find a way to stitch together hope.

And so, I joined forces with Mr. Rajan, my own limitations insignificant in comparison. Together, we embarked on a new chapter—one where compassion, courage, and the unwavering desire to serve would guide our steps. In the quiet corners of that small shop, I discovered that sometimes, the most profound transformations occur in the simplest acts of kindness.

In a strong effort to support his hard work, I decided to find him. Recently, I learned that thieves had stolen his materials and broken the lock on his shop, making things even worse for him.

His life felt like a fragile thread—every time he tried to rise through hard work, he was pulled back down by tough circumstances.

Wanting to help him, I told him I would support him with our funds. He reacted with deep gratitude. Often, people in need are asked for surveys but receive no real help. He said he initially expected the same outcome this time but was happy to find that real kindness still exists.

This tough time in his life had almost taken away his belief in goodness, but our support renewed his faith, not just through financial aid but also by restoring his trust in the kindness that still exists.

His gratitude was overwhelming, showing the real power of support and encouragement. It reminded me that helping others is not just about giving money; it's about bringing hope and empowering people to create a better future for themselves and their communities. Through this act of generosity, I saw the strength of the human spirit and felt a strong connection with others. It made me realize how kindness can spread and foster empathy and understanding. By helping Mr. Rajan, I felt closer to the heart of humanity, where compassion matters most.

As I thought about our contribution, I realized our actions had sparked hope and possibility. I could see the change in Mr. Rajan's demeanor—his worries eased, replaced by a new sense of optimism. His gratitude, shown not just in words but also in the light in his eyes, reminded me of how a single act of kindness can deeply impact someone.

Our interaction also made me reflect on my own role in promoting kindness and empathy. It made me question the sincerity of my own promises and how committed I was to those values. It's easy to talk about high ideals, but our true beliefs are shown in our actions, no matter how small.

In the end, my encounter with Mr. Rajan became more than just a moment of charity; it turned into a journey of self-discovery and enlightenment.

After a few days, I revisited him, eager to witness the impact of our contribution on his budding enterprise. I wanted to ensure that our assistance had truly catalyzed positive change and had been directed towards its intended purpose. As I approached his humble establishment once more, a sense of anticipation mingled with hope filled my heart. Upon meeting him, his face lit up with genuine joy, eager to share the fruits of his labor since our last encounter.

He shared how he used the funds to buy a second-hand table and improve his small shop. His upgrades weren't just for looks; they were to make his livelihood more secure. He had cleverly strengthened his setup to prevent theft, ensuring his hard-earned materials were safe. Seeing his shop transformed filled me with pride, knowing our contribution provided him with a sense of security and peace of mind.

The fact that he could now sleep peacefully, knowing his business was protected, was incredibly rewarding. When I told him we would provide more support, his gratitude was overwhelming, showing the real power of kindness and encouragement.

After a few days, when I revisted his shop, he told me how he had managed and used the 2nd instalment wisely. He bought packets of Kurkure, Lays Chips, and stock of chocolates and other snacks to sell so that he could attract more customers and earn more profit, ensuring his situation didn't betray him. He also shared how our funds had helped him a lot; through the first installment, he repaired his shop, and through the second, he stocked materials so that his business could continue running in a stable manner.

"*Our shared journey showed me that even small acts of kindness can brighten the darkest places, weaving hope into the fabric of humanity.*"

CHAPTER SEVEN

GENEROSITY AND GROWTH

-By Kanchan Kol

I remember my experience with our first book. It helped me understand the age-old questions: What is poverty, and why do people beg? Through that journey, I learned the importance of empathy for others.

This time, I have a story about a vegetable vendor to share. What do you think are some common problems that vegetable sellers face? Price fluctuations and investing in their business are definitely common challenges.

Mr. Gautam Kumar

For three weeks, I'd been seeing a vegetable vendor at the market. He always worked hard, but his stall seemed to be getting emptier each time I stopped by. He looked sad and discouraged. I wanted to know what was wrong, so I asked him.

At first, he didn't want to talk about it, but he eventually opened up to me. He told me he had sold something precious to get some money for his business. But the prices of vegetables were going up, so people weren't buying much. He was losing money and didn't know what to do. He said he was thinking of closing his shop and begging on the street to survive. It was clear he was really struggling.

I knew I wanted to help him. I decided to interview him for our project, and I asked him what he would do with some money if we could give it to him. He said he wanted to buy more vegetables and some tools to make his business better. He was only selling green leafy vegetables because he couldn't afford tomatoes and other things. He dreamed of expanding his shop and having more to sell. He and his wife work hard to support their family of four, but they have two children studying in their village because they can't afford school in Pune. Their biggest wish is to give their kids a good education and a better life.

A few days later, I returned to the shop. The uncle's face lit up with a huge smile, one of the happiest I'd ever seen. Looking into his eyes, I could see a glimmer of hope, a belief that things might actually get better. It made me realize that everyone deserves this kind of happiness, but sadly, life often throws obstacles in our way.

He accepted the money with deep gratitude, understanding the importance of the support we were offering. He planned to use the money to expand his business and buy more vegetables. He was incredibly thankful and truly appreciated the help we had given him.

After a few days, I revisited the shop. I approached my uncle to ask what had happened and what changes they had made. He explained that he had invested a significant portion of the money in leafy vegetables, with a smaller amount allocated to other varieties. This was due to his recent venture into diversifying his produce to mitigate potential losses. Despite his initial cautious approach, he expressed satisfaction with the trajectory of his business and foresaw potential growth with continued success. He gratefully acknowledged my empathy and support, recognizing that the expansion of his business wouldn't have been possible without my assistance. He conveyed his heartfelt appreciation for the opportunity.

I visited the shop again, and this time, the uncle's wife was there. She was surprised because I had already helped them once before, and now I was giving them more funds. She got emotional, her eyes filled with tears, and she thanked me for helping them build a better future for their children and grow their businesses. She was so grateful for my trust and kindness. With this money, they could expand their business, and they hoped to be able to send their children to a better school in Pune if things went well.

A few weeks later, I went back to the shop and noticed that the uncle had completely changed things. His stall was overflowing with vegetables, and people were buying from him! He looked happy. He told me he had used the money to buy more vegetables, especially for Makar Sankranti, a special time when people in Maharashtra buy specific kinds of vegetables. The investment had paid off, and he even made enough money to send some back to his village for his children. I was happy for him and told him to keep working hard to improve his business. He was smart with his money and didn't waste a penny.

He was a bit surprised to see me so late and asked why I hadn't been around. I told him I'd been busy with college, but that I was still committed to helping him grow. And bid him goodbye.

While writing this story, I realized that,

"Trust, kindness, and empathy are the keys to solving problems. When people show these qualities, they can help themselves and others."

CHAPTER EIGHT

FLOWERS OF DESPAIR

-By Sanskruti Badgujar

Our previous book not only imparted numerous skills but also prompted us to question societal norms. It made me realize that growing up in poverty, enduring abuse, living in a violent community, hailing from a broken home, and lacking positive role models are formidable challenges. Despite these adversities, individuals strive to survive in a harsh society, which, in my opinion, is among the most daunting experiences one can endure.

I remember my friend's interview with Mrs. Rani, whose story of struggles I read. It was clear she needed help after hearing her story. However, when we tried to interview her again two years later, she refused, expressing her frustration with the process. She felt sharing her experiences again would be dishonest, highlighting the deep distrust felt by many in similar situations.

It was a little difficult for us to convince her, but we explained everything to make her understand that it was true that someone was standing there to help them.

Mrs. Rani Chavan with her kids

Mrs. Rani Chavan, the subject of my interview, navigates life by planning and buying goods in accordance with seasonal demands. With four children, two residing in a hostel and the other two staying home without attending school, the entire family pitches in to work alongside their parents. Witnessing their living conditions firsthand revealed the stark reality of their hardship.

During our conversation, Mrs. Chavan's words broke my heart and struck a chord when she expressed that,

"अगर हम एक भी दिन ये बेचने नही जाए, तो घर में खाना नही पकेगा।"

(Even if one day we do not sell these things, we will not be able to cook food at home). Compounded by her husband's prolonged illness and the resulting hospital bills, it became evident that financial support was urgently required.

I explored the significant aspects of her life, including her decision to live in a slum area and the challenges she faces despite not having a proper home. It was heartbreaking for me to see her struggle without shelter while others had protection from harsh weather like heat or rain.

It was covered with a makeshift yellow plastic material, and the room was open with no doors. Seeing this saddened me, and I couldn't stop wondering how difficult it must be to live in such conditions. It's hard to imagine their daily struggles. While some might cry or feel tense over small issues, these people face much bigger challenges every day. Their resilience and ability to endure such hardships is truly remarkable.

The next day, when I approached her, she gave me a big smile with a kind look. She thought we were just passing by, so she didn't say anything to me and went to a traffic signal to sell her goods. Then I immediately called her and told her that I wanted to hand over the money to her. At first, she didn't believe we would give her the money. There were happy tears in her eyes, and it made me emotional as well.

A few days later, I approached her and inquired about what she had purchased with the money. She replied that she had bought some items for resale, and she even showed me the merchandise.

After a few days, I returned to her house with some help. It was a sunny morning when I left home, but it wasn't the same for her. When I got there, she wasn't home. While walking back, I saw her on a path and stopped to talk. She looked tense, so I asked how she was doing and mentioned I had been to her house. She said, "I had to go to the hospital because my husband was sick." In that moment, I realized that even though I was having a nice day, she was going through a lot of pain. Her sadness was clear on her face. Despite her worries, she spoke to me kindly, and it warmed my heart.

Then I handed over the second instalment. Aunty couldn't believe it; she was shocked. This time, she was quite happy and looked at me with thankful eyes.

I thought the money could be useful in the hospital. She said, "You've helped us; we're immensely thankful." After everything, I felt that I had neither helped the wrong person nor given money to the wrong hands.

I realised responsibility and poverty play very important roles in everyone's life, especially for poor people. If someone asks, tell them the spelling of responsibility, we can spell it out easily, but its meaning is so deep. When responsibility comes, a person becomes ready to work hard and do whatever is required. That's why I felt that poverty and circumstances make a person mature before their time.

With the second instalment, I was surprised to see that she used the money to build a house. I got curious and asked her, "It takes a lot of money to build a house, so how did you do it?" She said that she made some profit from the money given to her the first time and saved that money. It was profit money from the initial Rs 3000, which she saved, and she added some more money from the second instalment. From that, she built a house. I am happy that now at least she has a small house, and the house is much better than the first one.

Her House

I would just like to end by saying,

"Even a small gesture from you can bring a smile to someone's face."

CHAPTER NINE

BEYOND THE STREET

-By Pooja Bodekar

As I continued my journey with the book project, my enthusiasm only grew. Meeting new people and listening to their stories filled me with joy. Though the initial encounters had been intimidating, the lessons learned prepared me for the unknown ahead. I was determined to connect with strangers and bring their voices to life.

During my search for someone truly in need, I met a shopkeeper near Pune Station. I excitedly explained our project. However, he declined, saying, "If I ever decide to expand my business, I'll take a loan instead of accepting your help." He was polite but firm, making it clear he wanted to remain self-sufficient. After several similar rejections, I felt disheartened but refused to give up.

Then, I spotted a vegetable seller. I approached him, hoping to hear his story. Initially hesitant, he soon opened up after I explained our project aimed at helping people like him. He praised young people for caring and said, "You're making a difference." I felt proud to be part of a project that aimed to uplift others.

One of the most impactful encounters was with Mr. Nana Valke, a dedicated fruit vendor near the Pune Station bus stop. He shared his reasons for choosing fruits over vegetables: "Less waste, less loss." As I explained our mission, his eyes lit up with curiosity. "Why would you help us?" he asked, his voice filled with gratitude. I assured him of our genuine intentions, and he opened up about his dreams and challenges. He accepted our assistance, promising to use it wisely, saying, "This money will help me expand my business."

Mr. Nana Valke

When I returned later, I was pleased to see his progress. He had used the funds to bring in fresh fruits, and his business was flourishing. However, as I observed his success, doubts crept in. Was he truly in need of assistance, or had I chosen the wrong person to help? While his story embodied the resilience of everyday heroes striving to make ends meet, I began to question if my support could have had a more significant impact elsewhere. By sharing their struggles and strengths, we honored their lives, but I couldn't shake the feeling that I might have missed an opportunity to help someone truly in need. This realization prompted me to start looking for another person.

One day, near my home in Manjri, I met Uncle Aana, our daily vegetable vendor. He lived in Ghule Nagar with his family of five and was struggling to make ends meet. His difficulties touched my heart. Uncle Aana's small shop needed expansion, and our aid could be a lifeline. When I offered help, his face lit up with joy. "Thank you!" he exclaimed, promising to use the funds wisely. Seeing Uncle Aana's gratitude reinforced my belief in our mission.

Mr. Aana

After a few days, I checked in on Uncle Aana. He had wisely used the money to buy vegetables and was earning a profit. With his new earnings, he paid his rent, beaming with happiness. Uncle Aana's eyes sparkled with pride, not just for himself but for us. "You young ones are helping us, understanding our struggles," he said. Our compassion had touched his heart.

In that moment, we shared a deep connection. I saw the impact of our actions, and Uncle Aana realized his struggles mattered. Our small act of kindness renewed his hope. Uncle Aana's smile reflected the power of human connection, reminding us that everyone's story deserves to be heard.

Reflecting on my journey, I realized that helping Uncle Aana and Nana wasn't just about giving money; it was about connection, empathy, and understanding. We often overlook the struggles of those around us, but every story deserves to be heard. Our small acts of kindness can awaken hope and renew faith in humanity.

Part III: Tales of Local Heroes

FROM UNCERTAINTY TO HOPE

-By Nitesh Yadav

Mr. Hanmant Rau Jadhav

When I went to Mr Hanmant Rau Jadhav, he seemed a bit unsure at first. He thought I wanted to buy something from him. But when I explained that I wasn't there to buy, but to help, he relaxed a bit. He looked interested, but also tired, like life had been tough on him. Mr. Hanmant sold things near Shaniwar Wada, where it was always noisy because of the traffic. He had trouble walking, so he used a wheelchair. He didn't have a home, so he slept on the street where he sold his things. His clothes were old and worn out, showing that he didn't have an easy life. As he told me about himself, it was clear he had been through a lot. He lost his family in a bad accident, and it still hurt him to talk about it. But he was tough, and he kept going. When I mentioned our project, he seemed hopeful. He was glad for the chance to tell his story and to get some help for his small business.

Finally, the long-awaited day arrived when I could hand over the first instalment to Mr. Hanmant. It wasn't just a financial transaction; it was a moment filled with emotion and purpose. Despite having met him several times since our initial interview, this encounter felt different. As I set out in the morning, eager yet nervous, I couldn't locate him. It wasn't until later, on my way home from college, that I spotted him. His smile seemed to convey a sense of anticipation as if he knew I was coming. Approaching him, I felt a surge of pride and warmth as I handed over the money. It was more than just a monetary gift; it was a gesture of compassion and support, a small beacon of hope in his challenging circumstances.

With the 3000 rupees in hand, Mr. Hanmant quickly put the money to good use. Instead of just buying things to resell, he thought carefully about how to invest it to better his situation. While he focused on earphones, he also saved some for emergencies, showing his ability to plan ahead.

As I reflected on the encounter, I couldn't help but feel a renewed sense of purpose. It was a humbling reminder that,

> "*Sometimes, the greatest impact we can have is not measured in monetary terms but in the depth of*

compassion and empathy we show towards others. "

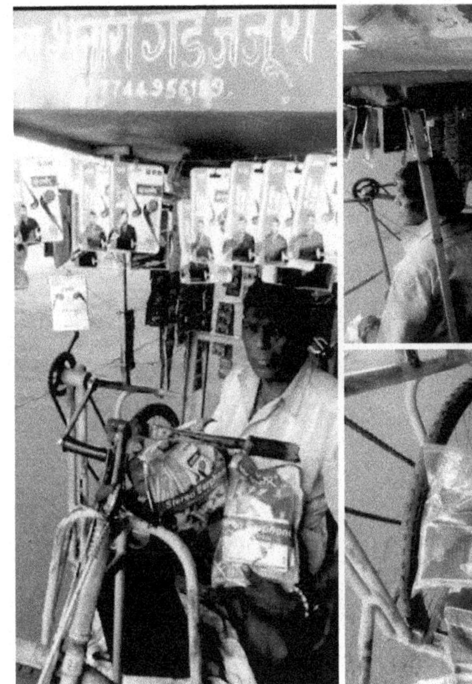

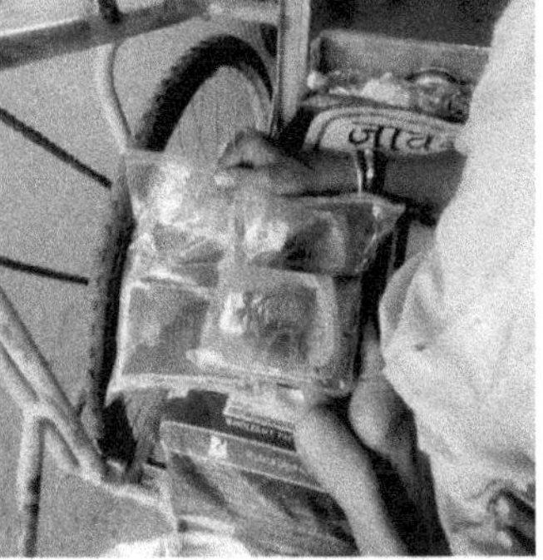

After following up on the progress since the first instalment, it was time to reach out for another. When he saw me approaching, his face lit up with a hopeful smile. Before handing over the money, I asked him how things were going and if our support was making a difference. He shared that our assistance was keeping his spirits high and motivating him to work harder despite the challenges. He admitted feeling anxious about the second instalment, as it was crucial for expanding his business and securing a better future. But when I finally gave him the money, he thanked us profusely for standing by him and trying to ease his burdens.

When I visited him next week, he proudly showed me the items he purchased with the second instalment – USB cables, earphones, and other essentials. Some of these items were already displayed on his wheelchair for sale, indicating his determination to earn a livelihood. This time, he utilized every rupee wisely, investing it in products that could help sustain him and his business.

He was deeply grateful for the assistance, acknowledging how this small step had brightened his life. Now, with a means to earn his sustenance and a glimpse of hope for a stable future, he felt profoundly touched by our support. As we concluded our conversation, he posed a heartfelt question: Why were we helping him? Though it was difficult to articulate, I recounted our journey, from the inception of our first book to our encounters with individuals like him. His face lit up with appreciation, knowing that we had taken the time to understand their struggles and extend a helping hand.

Reflecting on my journey, I remembered the initial apprehension and doubts I faced when reaching out to people and earning their trust. Yet, drawing strength from past experiences and the encouragement of my mentor and co-authors, I persevered. Despite the challenges, completing this task brought me immense joy, pride, and a profound sense of fulfilment, knowing that our efforts were shaping a brighter future for someone in need.

From Struggles to Sustainability

-By Aarti Sharma

Mr. Aatish Pawar

He is Mr. Aatish Pawar, whom my classmate interviewed in the previous book. I decided to interview him as I already knew about his struggles and what he has been facing since childhood.

I hesitated a bit since it was two years ago when my classmate interviewed him, but now it was time to help. I was a bit nervous about whether he would believe me.

After a lot of self-pushing, I asked him, 'Uncle, क्या मैं आपसे कुछ बात कर सकती हूँ?' (Can I talk to you for a minute?)

He agreed, and I asked him about his childhood struggles and why he's living in a slum area. He started sharing about his life; he was an orphan from a young age. He used to beg on the streets for a living. The police used to hit him just because he was begging. He didn't remember much. Currently, he is living in Pune, Keshav Nagar, in a slum area, and his house is fully made of bamboo and carpets; he has no door. I could sense the pain of living in this house without essential things.

He does not have a proper job; he sells different kinds of things like garbage bags, *gajra* (flower garlands), small toys, badges, wigs, and many more items on the street. Still, it's not sufficient for his family as there are 4-5 members in his family, and with such a limited range of products, he does not earn enough money to support them.

After hearing about all the challenges he was facing, I felt compelled to offer him some financial support.

I took the time to explain where the money was coming from and why I felt the need to help him. His eyes lit up with gratitude, and he nodded eagerly, a warm smile spreading across his face.

Curious about his plans, I gently inquired, "*Uncle,* What will you do with this money?" He paused, as if pondering the possibilities, before replying, "मैं इन पैसों से बेचने के लिए कुछ सामान लूंगा जैसे कि गार्बेज बैग्स, गजरा, वग्सि, और बहुत कुछ।" (I will buy some items to sell with this money, such as garbage bags, gajra, wigs, and much more.)

His words painted a picture of determination as he shared his intention to invest to grow his small business. It was a moment of hope and possibility.

A few days later, I visited him again to give him the money. His joy upon seeing me was on an extreme level; he was delighted. As I handed him the Rs 3000, his happiness knew no bounds. Both he and his wife showered me with blessings, expressing their gratitude for my kindness. Her repeated thanks touched me deeply. Witnessing his happiness brought me immense joy as well. The smile on his face was priceless.

A few days later, when I went to see him again, I asked, "Uncle, did you buy the things you wanted to sell?" He nodded, showing me the toys. I felt really happy knowing he hadn't wasted the money, and it made me trust him even more.

After a couple of days, when I visited him again, he was overjoyed to see me. He was surprised and didn't expect another Rs 3000 from me. But when he got the money, he was really thankful. He kept saying, "Thank you so much for your help." His whole family thanked me too, and it felt great to see them happy.

Since I saw him spending the last money wisely, I trusted him again. He proudly told me that with the profit from the money I gave him, he bought flags and badges for Republic Day. After a couple of days, I visited him again, he had bought many things like wigs, tiaras, face masks, and a few toys as well. I was happy that he used it in a careful way for his own growth and sustainability, and that made me believe that a little help provided to the right person can change their life.

It's so nice to see how much things have changed for him since I helped him out. He's been able to make some money by selling the things I gave him, so he won't be out of work anytime soon. And now, he can buy important items with the money he's earned. It's really making a big difference in his life.

After doing all this, I personally think that it was worth talking to him, it was worth giving him money. We always want more and more things; we are never satisfied with what we have. There are so many people who do not have a proper house to live and no good lifestyle, yet they are happy and working hard. So, one of my learnings is to be happy with what I have and work hard to achieve success. And my final learning is,

"Helping one person may not transform the entire world, but it can certainly change everything for that individual."

Part IV: Small Business Successes

CHAPTER TWELVE

PATH OF LIFE ISN'T EASY

-By Anushka Mishra

Mr Chanderpal Singh

In the first book, I wrote about Mr Chanderpal Singh. He is a Panipuri seller. He came to Pune with his family as he was unable to survive in Uttar Pradesh due to a lack of employment. He couldn't find any job that could help him and his family survive there. He came here with lots of hope but was unable to find any proper job. He was struggling with financial issues. As he could cook really well, he decided to set up a Panipuri stall.

In the initial stage, he struggled a lot. He faced many problems like people not eating his Panipuri, not talking to him properly, and even using bad words for small mistakes. In short, they were disrespecting him in many ways. He didn't lose hope and kept working harder. Every morning, he started working with new hopes that he would be able to manage everything with the same energy. He never thought of giving up. He kept trying harder and kept improving himself. After struggling for six years, his life was much better.

Now that we have received funds to help the people we interviewed in the first book, I was excited, happy, and nervous at the same time. It was pretty clear that I was going to help Chanderpal Bhaiya. I thought it wouldn't be a difficult task as I have a good relationship with him and had interviewed him before.

Due to my good relationship, it was easy to approach him, but convincing him was a bit hard. When I went back to him and told him everything about our book and how, after reading it, someone is ready to give funds and help out, he was sceptical.

I asked him what he would do with the money. He said that he would use it to repair his stall. He was still facing financial issues as he had borrowed money to start the business. Because of this, he couldn't repair his small setup. Small parts of the stall were broken, and the utensils seemed old, making it appear unhygienic. People again started avoiding his Panipuri, affecting his business.

Until I told him that someone was actually helping him, he thought it was fake and that I was joking. But I assured him that he could trust me and that we were genuinely going to help him as much as we could. After that, I could see clear happiness on his face. He was happy, but more than happiness, I could see more questions and fear. I asked him to tell me all his queries so that I could clear them up. Then he asked if he took the money, would we ask for anything in return? And if he spent the money and then we asked for it back, what would he do? Similar questions came up. I clarified his doubts and told him that once I gave him the money, it would be his as long as he used it properly and didn't misuse it. No one would ask for the money back as long as he used it correctly. He didn't have to be scared. So, I asked him to be happy and wait for me to come back with the first instalment.

After collecting the first instalment, I went to the Panipuri vendor that same evening to give it to him. It was a totally different experience. I felt happy and nervous at the same time. When I gave him the money, he was happy but unable to express it, and I could see the nervousness on his face. He was unsure about the money and still scared. But he was happy that someone was there to help him. He gave me lots of blessings. I feel lucky that I was able to help someone.

Then I asked him what he would do with that money. He said, "With that money, I will buy some utensils and repair the stall."

After some days, when I revisited him, I saw that he had repaired his stall and bought new utensils. The happiness I felt at that moment, after seeing his face, was just amazing, and I really felt connected to his life.

After a few weeks, I went towards his stall. This time, I was confident, and I could see a smile on his face on seeing me. When I started talking, he offered me a plate of Panipuri, but I declined because I didn't want to have it for free. If I wanted it, I would pay for it. But he was so kind.

Then I gave him the second instalment. He said to me, "Trust me, I will use it properly this time as well. I will not break your trust."

After hearing this, I was happy and felt proud that I was able to make someone believe in themselves and the people around them who are willing to help. This time, he was going to use the money to repair the actual stall and paint it.

After a few days, I got a message from my Uncle with a few pics of his stall which upgraded to a brand new look and feel. He had changed the broken parts of the stall and also painted it. He was happy, and this made me feel so blessed and proud.

A few days later, when I visited him, he told me that after the upgrades to the stall, the number of customers had increased. He thanked me and gave me lots of blessings. This journey taught me that

"*We may not be able to help everyone in need, but starting with just one person makes a meaningful difference.*"

BEYOND THE TIN ROOF

-By Suhani Dwivedi

Mrs. Pooja Karande

During my interaction with Mrs Pooja Karande, I delved into her life journey, discovering the many hurdles she faced. She talked about her simple upbringing with her family of five, which included her three children, her sick husband, and her mother-in-law. Her husband couldn't work due to his health, so she had to take care of everything with what little they had. Tears filled Mrs. Pooja's eyes as she talked about their financial troubles. Even though she was determined, they could only afford to send one of her three children to school. It was tough for her to decide because she knew her other two children couldn't pursue their dreams due to a lack of money.

As Mrs Pooja shared her story, she described their home in Keshav Nagar, made entirely of tin. It showed how they lived day by day, never knowing if they might lose their home. The fear of being evicted was always there, hanging over their heads like a dark cloud. She worked at her small shop with determination, being a source of hope for her family. Every sale she made demonstrated her strength, even when things were tough. As our conversation ended, I was amazed by her resilience. Even with all the hardships she faced, she kept going, hoping for a brighter future. Her story showed how powerful people can be, even when things seem impossible.

After hearing her story and seeing her strength, I decided to help her. I gave her some money to support her family. When she took it, her eyes lit up, giving her a bit of hope in tough times.

I asked, "Aunty, What will you do with it?" She said, "I'll use this money to buy goods and groceries for my shop." Her words showed how determined she was to make her shop thrive, even when times were tough. She promised to follow my advice and assured me that she would invest every penny carefully to help her small business grow. As our conversation ended, a hopeful and grateful vibe filled the air.

After a few days, when I approached Mrs. Pooja, I could sense she was a bit nervous, maybe because of all the uncertainty she was facing. But when I mentioned helping her out with money, I saw a spark of hope in her eyes. She was truly thankful, silently showing how much it meant to her to have some help when things were tough.

At first, she hesitated because she was worried about her husband's drinking problem. She feared that if we gave her money, he might use it for alcohol instead of helping the family. It was a sad moment that highlighted the heavy responsibility she felt for her family's future.

My friend Sanskruti kindly offered to keep the money safe until the next day, understanding Mrs. Pooja's concerns. It was a small but meaningful gesture, showing support and bringing together care and practical help in an instant.

As I observed Mrs. Pooja's reluctance to accept the money right away, I was deeply moved. It demonstrated her honesty and dedication to using the money wisely. Her decision to wait until she could ensure its proper use highlighted her kind nature, reminding me of the goodness in people.

The next day, I saw Mrs. Pooja using the first part of the money to restock her shop with important items. Seeing her carefully selecting chocolates, chips, eggs, and biscuits filled me with hope.

As I assured her I'd bring more money later, she was incredibly thankful. Her sincere words of gratitude reminded me how much a little help can mean to someone. With a sense of purpose, I bid her goodbye, knowing we'd meet again, connected by kindness and support.

When I gave her the second part of the money, she couldn't believe it. Tears filled her eyes as she saw the money, a sign of hope in her tough life. I reassured her that this was real and that we were there to help her.

With shaky hands, she took the money, overflowing with gratitude. It was a moment where giving meant so much more than just money—it was about connecting and caring for each other.

She thanked me sincerely for the help. It seemed like a weight had lifted off her shoulders, replaced by hope. I promised that I would come back soon to see how she was doing. It was a silent promise to support her.

With the second part of the funds, her shop thrived. It was filled with groceries, eggs, and other important items, attracting customers from all over. The change was evident, showing how kindness can make a big difference in someone's life. Her shop became a little more crowded, bringing in more money and easing her financial worries. This stability helped her family, making life easier for them. But the biggest change was in what she could now dream of. With her business doing well, she could think about sending all her kids to school, something she couldn't imagine before.

Reflecting on how we helped Mrs. Pooja, I feel proud. Her story is a reminder of how compassion can change lives, and it brings me happiness to be part of that change.

CHAPTER FOURTEEN

COMPASSION AND CHANGE

-By Saurabh Verma

One day, my mom asked me to buy some vegetables from the market. I went to the market and visited several vegetable shops. I was curious about the lives of the shopkeepers, so I asked them a few questions. But most of them just told me to leave because they were busy and didn't have time to chat.

I kept looking for a shop, and then I saw a small one that wasn't very busy. There weren't many vegetables there compared to the other shops. The shopkeeper looked sad, so I decided to talk to him. I asked him about himself, his life, and how he was doing.

He was polite, but I felt sorry for him when he said, "It's okay. You are very young, and you won't be able to help me."

I asked him, "Please tell me about yourself. I really want to know. Even if I can't help, maybe there are others who can. But we need to understand your situation first."

Mr. Vikas Kumar

The shopkeeper agreed to share his story. He told me that he had recently started selling vegetables. He used to be a security guard, but after his father passed away suddenly, he returned to his village to take care of his family. It took a long time for them to recover from the loss. When he came back to Pune, he had lost his job because he had been away for too long. He couldn't find another job due to his limited education, so he decided to start his own business with the little money he had left. A friend suggested selling vegetables. His family is poor, and he is the only one working to support them.

As he told his story, he got emotional. I felt sad, too. He seemed to be carrying a heavy weight. I decided I had to help him. I told him, "I will help you." He asked, "How?" I explained everything.

After a few days, I went back to the same market. The shopkeeper was still there, selling vegetables. I told him some good news—that his life was about to change. He was surprised and asked how. I told him that I was going to help him improve his business and his life. He said, "How will you help me improve my business?" I reminded him of our conversation and I promised to help him. I apologized and explained that I had been busy getting the money for him, but I had finally gotten it. He was so grateful and thanked me a lot. I told him the money was for him to use and to make his business better. He promised to use it for his business and not for anything else.

After a few days, I revisited the Uncle's shop, and he revealed that he had initiated a fruit-selling venture, with his wife handling the vegetable sales. She was assisting him. He further said, "With your money, I bought fruits and *thela*(vegetable cart)."

He was feeling very happy and proud of me because, from a young age, I had started helping deprived people and writing books. He offered me *papaya* to eat and told me that I could take whatever I needed from vegetables or fruits, but I told him "No" because this project was to help deprived people and not to accept their favour. He expressed gratitude, saying, 'You have changed my life.'

When I gave the uncle his second instalment, he was so happy he started to cry! He told me he had bought some vegetables, carrots, a scale for weighing, and other things he needed for his business. He had rented everything before, but now he was able to buy things. I was so glad to be helping someone who really needed it. You can see in the picture how happy he was to receive the money. I'm happy he's using it wisely for his needs, which will help him a lot in the future.

I asked him about his life and how he had achieved things. He said he had faced many challenges and had to work very hard to overcome them. He started working when he was only in the ninth grade, so he had to leave school. He worked in a village at first, but he didn't make much money, so he moved to the city to find better work.

When I went back to see how he was doing, he said,

"My business is doing much better now because of you and your friends. I'm glad you came and interviewed me and then gave me the money. It helped a lot."

He said that he was able to buy a lot more vegetables now, like potatoes, eggplant, tomatoes, ginger, and garlic.

When I went to interview different vegetable sellers, many of them yelled at me. But this man didn't. He had real problems, and he shared them with me because he felt comfortable talking to me. I learnt that we should try to make people feel comfortable, that's when they open up and share their heart out.

CHAPTER FIFTEEN

Pouring Changes in the Cup

-By Shraddha Singh

We often think that poverty means only being hungry, wearing ragged clothes, and being homeless. But poverty is much more than that. It also means being unloved, uncared for, and unwanted by society.

In our previous book, "**The Unheard Voices of Mundhwa**," we saw the harsh realities of society. Collecting stories showed us the need for help, but we struggled with how to offer it. This project finally gave us a way to support those whose stories we shared.

On my journey, I met a cobbler uncle and shared details about our previous book, asking if he would agree to an interview. He kindly consented, and during our conversation, I gently asked, "If we gave you some money to help, how would it change your life?" His heartfelt response moved me deeply; he expressed a desire to change his job and become a fruit seller, adding, "कम से कम थोड़ी इज़्जत तो मिलेगी" (at least I'll have some respect). His words touched me profoundly, sparking an immediate urge to assist him.

As I made my way back to him, I was filled with hope and excitement, eager to present a proposal that could slightly improve his life and provide sustainability. However, after several discussions, he ultimately rejected my proposal, shattering my enthusiasm. "I'm sorry, I don't need any help," he murmured softly. Confused, I couldn't help but ask, "But why?" Despite my persistent inquiries, he didn't provide a clear answer. It struck me that trust is rare, especially between strangers—and to him, I was just that. Growing up, we are taught to avoid interactions with strangers and to be cautious of accepting their help. It baffled me that he could not trust a young stranger like me with a substantial amount of money, despite my best efforts to convince him. This left me feeling disheartened.

A few days later, I resumed my search for someone who could genuinely benefit from our assistance and encountered another elderly cobbler uncle. After explaining the context and asking the same question, he replied, "मैं इन पैसों को घर के लिए उपयोग करूंगा, बिजिनेस में लगा कर कुछ फायदा नहीं हो क्योंकि जब तक आप लोगों के चप्पल या जूते खराब नहीं होते, आप हमारे पास नहीं आओगे, तो बिजिनेस में लगा कर भी सिर्फ नुक़सान ही होगा और अगर पैसे लेने ही हैं तो मैं बैंक से लोन ले लूंगा" (I will use this money for household needs only. Investing it in my business wouldn't yield any benefits, as customers only come when their footwear needs repair. It would only lead to losses. If I need funds, I'll opt for a bank loan). His honest response left me feeling both pleased and disheartened; while I didn't secure the interview I sought,

I found comfort in his remarkable honesty. He spoke the truth that resided within him without hesitation.

I made two attempts to find someone to help, both of which ended in disappointment. Doubts clouded my mind, but my heart urged me to try one more time—a thought that was both hopeful and exciting. With determination, I set out on a final quest, thinking of the tea seller near Pune station, a familiar sight from my college bus rides. His roadside stall was always busy, with the enchanting aroma of his tea attracting passersby like bees to flowers. This made me realize that our identity is shaped more by the meaningful work we do than by what we own. I often found myself gazing longingly at his stall as my bus stopped at the signal, captivated by how gracefully he prepared his tea. It was a scene that always filled me with curiosity and admiration.

However, amidst the chaos of college life, I never found the time to stop for a cup of his tea, a regret that lingered in my heart. Yet now, this missed opportunity felt like a second chance. Maybe I had never visited his shop for a reason, and now everything was leading to this moment where my path could finally intersect with his.

As I headed to interview him for our book, I felt a mix of excitement and anxiety. What if he refused to share his story? That thought dampened my enthusiasm. The next day, as I boarded the bus, I practiced my questions, preparing myself for the encounter. With a renewed sense of purpose, I stood in front of his stall once more. The aroma of his tea enveloped me, igniting a spark of excitement within. I watched him move with practiced ease, his hands gracefully preparing each cup with care—a true dance of passion and pride in his work.

Amidst the crowd, I gathered the courage to approach him, softly asking, "*Uncle,* क्या मैं आपसे दो मिनट बात कर सकती हूँ?" (Could I have just two minutes of your time?)

His crowd of customers closed in, causing a brief delay, during which I got some more time to prepare myself. When he finally granted me an audience, I felt a surge of nervous energy. "I'm not here to ask for help," I clarified, catching him off guard.

"Oh? Then what brings you here?" he inquired, his curiosity provoked.

With conviction, I explained our previous project to him, illustrating how his participation would be mutually beneficial for himself. Having laid out our interview proposal comprehensively, I succeeded in fostering a sense of trust, prompting his willingness to engage. During our discussion, I casually inquired how he might utilize a potential Rs 6000 assistance. His response carried a genuine emotional weight, as he spoke of his earnest intentions to invest in the growth of his tea shop and provide for his family's needs.

Mr Jadhav

He is Mr Jadhav, a tea seller whose tea smells so amazing that it can draw anyone in with its wonderful aroma. During our conversation, he mentioned his family. Mr Jadhav has a large family with about 10 people, including his mom, dad, older brother, sister-in-law, his wife, and their children. Having a large family in today's world is both a blessing and a challenge. While the sense of togetherness and support is invaluable, it also brings its own set of difficulties. With the ever-increasing expenses, managing the needs of a big family becomes more challenging, adding to the complexity of daily life.

Within a few days, I made my way back to him to deliver the needed money. As I approached him once more, a hint of disbelief flickered across his face, drawing my focus. It was as if he couldn't fathom that someone would step forward to alleviate his struggles. His expression transformed into one of sheer delight and gratitude when I handed over the money to him. Every heartfelt word of thanks he shared filled my heart with warmth, echoing within me and bringing a sense of profound satisfaction.

Witnessing the transformation on his face, from disbelief to sheer happiness, brought a profound sense of fulfilment to my soul. Despite the fact that the money came from another source, I couldn't help but feel a swell of happiness knowing that I had played a part in bringing that radiant smile to his face.

In that moment of gratitude and joy, Mr Jadhav said,

"मैं आप सभी का आभारी हूँ आपकी मदद के लिए और उसके लिए भी कि आपने अपना समय नकिालकर मुझे यहाँ तक पहुँचाया और मदद की। मैं आपके शकि्षक और आपके बाकी लोगों से भी मलिना और उनका धन्यवाद करना चाहता हूँ"

(I am grateful to all of you, for your assistance and for taking the time out of your schedule to come here and help me. I also want to meet and express my gratitude to your teacher and other members of your team.)

His eyes sparkled with joy, yet there was a hint of emotion in his voice as he expressed his gratitude. I emphasized that receiving the second instalment depended on his prudent use of the first. With a solemn nod, he accepted my condition, placing his trust in me to utilize the funds wisely and diligently for his advancement.

When I returned to him to see his progress, I struggled to locate him in his usual spot for quite some time. My college schedule meant I arrived earlier than his workday typically started, leaving me to wonder if he had moved to some other place. However, one day on my way to college, I chanced upon him once more and seized the opportunity to inquire about his progress. The sight of him instantly offering me a cup of tea filled me with a profound sense of gratitude. At that moment, I felt truly blessed by his kindness.

As we sat together, he eagerly explained to me how our assistance brought a few small changes in his life. He said that he had invested in a new gas stove and cylinder, anticipating it would lead to greater efficiency in his work. Recognizing his responsible use of the funds, I decided to provide him with the second instalment without hesitation.

With the additional funds, he purchased more food items to complement his tea sales, as well as utensils and a large tea can. These seemingly mundane objects were far more than just materials to him; they were the lifeline that sustained him in this world. During our conversation, I couldn't help but inquire about the challenges he faced working alone, standing for hours on end, and making deliveries to nearby offices. His response, delivered with a radiant smile, revealed that he was not alone in his endeavours. His brother stood by his side, providing invaluable assistance and even managing the shop at times.

I was overwhelmed and deeply impressed by his words. In an age where sibling relationships often seem fraught with conflict or indifference, his bond with his brother was a shining example of support and solidarity.

It was a really touching moment that stuck with me, teaching me incredible lessons of life that I feel deep down inside. The main thing I learnt was that when we compare ourselves to others, it takes away how special our own journey is. Instead of craving for what others have, we should be thankful and work to make our lives better every day. We should aim to discover peace and happiness right where we are, in our own lives and surroundings.

And working together? It's like magic, this experience showed me how working together is so powerful. When we join forces, we can achieve great things and make the world a better place for everyone.

In the end, this journey has given me a new reason to keep going and have a deeper love for life's little joys. As Mother Teresa said, "Not all of us can do great things. But we can do small things with great love." And Maya Angelou wisely said,

> "*I've learned that people will forget what you said, people will forget what you did, but people will never forget how you made them feel.*"

Afterword

In shadows deep, where whispers lie,
Homeless dreams beneath the sky,
Roadside vendors, dawn to night,
Their struggles are hidden from our sight.

Vulnerable souls in quiet pain,
Enduring hardships, loss, and strain,
Yet in their eyes, a spark remains,
A glimmer through the endless rains.

We heard their voices, soft yet clear,
Their silent cries reached every ear,
With open hearts and willing hands,
We stood as one, made firm our stands.

Financial aid, a lifeline cast,
To lift them up, to hold them fast,
In unity, we found our way,
To turn their darkness into day.

Unheard voices, finally heard,
Stories shared, and hearts stirred,
No longer silent, voices rise,
Hope rekindled in their eyes.

Together strong, we made a stand,
Echoes of the streets, now hand in hand,
For every soul deserves to see,
A future bright, a life set free.

www.ingramcontent.com/pod-product-compliance
Lightning Source LLC
Chambersburg PA
CBHW040738120726
48007CB00008B/124